AF228558

INDIANA PACERS

BY WILL GRAVES

SportsZone

An Imprint of Abdo Publishing
abdobooks.com

abdobooks.com

Published by Abdo Publishing, a division of ABDO, PO Box 398166, Minneapolis, Minnesota 55439. Copyright © 2023 by Abdo Consulting Group, Inc. International copyrights reserved in all countries. No part of this book may be reproduced in any form without written permission from the publisher. SportsZone™ is a trademark and logo of Abdo Publishing.

Printed in China.
052022
092022

Cover Photo: Dylan Buell/Getty Images Sport/Getty Images
Interior Photos: Melinda Nagy/Shutterstock Images, 1; L.M. Otero/AP Images, 4; Eugene Garcia/AFP/Getty Images, 6; Bill Kostroun/AP Images, 9, 10; AP Images, 12, 25; Focus on Sport/Getty Images, 15; Jim Davis/Boston Globe/Getty Images, 17; David Santiago/El Nuevo Herald/Tribune News Service/Getty Images, 19; Dylan Buell/Getty Images Sport/ Getty Images, 20; George Gojkovich/Getty Images Sport/Getty Images, 22; Focus on Sport/Getty Images Sport/Getty Images, 26, 34; John Ruthroff/AFP/Getty Images, 29, 37; John Bazemore/AP Images, 30; Darron Cummings/AP Images, 32; Gina Ferazzi/Los Angeles Times/Getty Images, 38; Michael Conroy/AP Images, 40

Editor: Charlie Beattie
Series Designer: Joshua Olson

Library of Congress Control Number: 2021951670

Publisher's Cataloging-in-Publication Data

Names: Graves, Will, author.
Title: Indiana Pacers / by Will Graves
Description: Minneapolis, Minnesota : Abdo Publishing, 2023 | Series: Inside the NBA | Includes online resources and index.
Identifiers: ISBN 9781532198298 (lib. bdg.) | ISBN 9781098271947 (ebook)
Subjects: LCSH: Indiana Pacers (Basketball team)--Juvenile literature. | Basketball--Juvenile literature. | Professional sports--Juvenile literature. | Sports franchises--Juvenile literature.
Classification: DDC 796.32364--dc23

TABLE OF CONTENTS

CHAPTER ONE

REGGIE TIME

The Indiana Pacers appeared finished in Game 1 of the 1995 Eastern Conference semifinals. They trailed the rival New York Knicks by six points. And only 18 seconds were left on the clock. Even worse, star guard Reggie Miller was having an off day.

Miller was one of the best shooters in the National Basketball Association (NBA) during the 1990s. He had scored 23 points so far in Game 1. But he had struggled to hit shots. Miller was just 5-for-16 from the field, and he was 1-for-5 from three-point range. Most of his points had come from free throws. However, on this afternoon, the fearless shooting guard still had a trick up his sleeve.

The teams were meeting for the third consecutive year in the playoffs. New York had won each of the previous matchups. The 1993 series was in the first round. The Knicks brushed

Reggie Miller hoists a shot late in the 1995 Eastern Conference semifinals against the New York Knicks.

The Pacers and Knicks played in several physical playoff series during the 1990s.

Indiana aside in four games. In 1994 the Knicks had pulled out a 94–90 victory in Game 7 of the Eastern Conference finals. That came after a back-and-forth series between the bitter rivals. Now the Knicks were favored to make it three in a row.

The thought of losing to the Knicks again did not sit well with Pacers fans. The rivalry between the teams was heated on the court. The fans' rivalry was equally fierce off the court. Indiana fans felt that New Yorkers looked at them as country bumpkins. They wanted nothing more than to take down the team from the big city. Despite growing up in California, Miller embraced Indiana's underdog role. "There's nothing I want more than to beat [the Knicks] on their stage, to steal their show," Miller said. "I got great enjoyment from it."

A BRUISING CONTEST

Indiana believed it had enough to get past New York in 1995. But the rugged Knicks defense was giving Miller and his teammates a difficult time. The 6-foot-7, 185-pound Miller was struggling to find room to score. He missed seven of his first eight shots. Knicks big men Patrick Ewing and Charles Oakley took turns swatting Miller's attempts out of bounds.

The officials had a hard time keeping up with the game's physicality. They called a playoff record of 59 fouls. New York guard Derek Harper was tossed from the game after receiving his second technical foul. At one point, a shove sent Miller sprawling into the stands under the basket.

The crowd at New York's Madison Square Garden was on its feet as the fourth-quarter clock wound down. Their team up 105–99, the fans were eager

Smits Soars

While Reggie Miller saved the day in Game 1, he wasn't the only hero for the Pacers against the Knicks. Indiana center Rik Smits held his own against Patrick Ewing and the rugged New York defense. Smits averaged 22.6 points and 6.4 rebounds per game in the series. That included 34 points in Game 1. He fouled out late, however, setting the stage for Miller to take over.

to see the Knicks close out Game 1. That's when "Miller Time" truly began.

SHOOTING DISPLAY

Miller took an inbounds pass from Pacers point guard Mark Jackson. Quickly turning, he drilled a three-pointer from the wing to cut the lead to 105–102.

The Knicks still didn't need to panic. They just had to inbound the ball and wait to be fouled. But Knicks guard Greg Anthony slipped getting into position to receive a pass. Fearing a five-second inbound violation, teammate Anthony Mason threw the ball in anyway. It went right into Miller's hands. He coolly stepped back behind the three-point line and canned the game-tying basket. Madison Square Garden was stunned. Miller had erased the lead in six seconds.

The rest of the Pacers seemed to be stunned also. Pacers forward Sam Mitchell fouled New York's John Starks on the next inbounds pass. Now the Knicks had a chance to retake the lead. Starks stepped up to the line and was long on his first shot. He hit the front rim on his second shot. Ewing grabbed the rebound and attempted a short jumper. That missed too.

Miller muscled his way through two Knicks for the rebound of Ewing's miss. Then the whistle blew for a foul. Starks had grabbed Miller. The Pacers star would have a chance at the line.

The Knicks' John Starks reacts after missing two free throws late in Game 1 of the 1995 Eastern Conference semifinals.

Miller stares down the crowd at New York's Madison Square Garden after hitting his go-ahead shot.

Despite his shooting struggles from the field, Miller was his usual smooth self at the free throw line in Game 1. At that point he had made 12 of 13 foul shots. Shrugging off the pressure, he strolled up and knocked down two more. Just 8.9 seconds earlier on the game clock, the Pacers had trailed by six points. Now they led 107–105.

Famous film director Spike Lee was seated in the front row. All game long Miller had been talking trash with the Knicks superfan. Now Lee, and the rest of the crowd, sat in silence. New York still had time, but they were rattled. The Knicks didn't even get off a game-tying shot. Anthony fell while dribbling and the clock ran out. The Pacers had snatched a victory no one saw coming.

No one, that is, except Miller. Before the playoffs began, he said he wanted to face the Knicks. His wish was granted. Now he and his teammates were determined to make the most of it.

Miller said after Game 1 he wanted to sweep New York. That didn't happen, as the series went to seven games. But unlike the previous year, Indiana came through. Behind Miller's 29 points, the Pacers tipped New York 97–95 in the decisive seventh game. Indiana was back in the Eastern Conference finals, and Miller's nine seconds of magic paved the way.

PACERS
34
MIAM

SETTING THE PACE

Dr. James Naismith invented basketball in 1891. Just three years later, the sport arrived in Indiana. It didn't take long for hoops to catch on in the Hoosier State. For the next 50 years, basketball grew into an Indiana staple at the high school and college levels.

Men's professional basketball came to Indiana in the late 1940s. The Indianapolis Jets played in the Basketball Association of America (BAA). But as that league morphed into the NBA in 1949, the Jets folded. In their place came the Indianapolis Olympians. The new team in town lasted four seasons in the NBA before folding in 1953.

Two decades later, a group of Indianapolis businessmen wanted to get Indiana back in the pro game. The group decided to join a new league called the American Basketball Association (ABA). On February 2, 1967, the Indiana Pacers

Indiana's Mel Daniels battles for a rebound during a 1969 ABA game against the Miami Floridians.

were born. The owners chose the nickname to honor the pace cars that run ahead of the field at the Indianapolis 500 car race. It also nodded toward Indiana's long history with harness racing. In that sport, some of the horses that compete are called pacing horses, or "pacers."

The ABA was created to rival the NBA. The new league made a point to be as different as possible from the established league. The ABA used a red, white, and blue ball. They also introduced the three-point line and basketball's first dunk contest. Most importantly, the ABA wanted basketball to be fun and fast paced.

ABA DYNASTY

Few teams in basketball were more fun than the Pacers. Led by young stars Freddie Lewis, Roger Brown, and Mel Daniels, Indiana reached the ABA Finals in its second season. Unfortunately, the team's bid for a championship fell short. The Pacers lost to the Oakland Oaks 4–1 in the best-of-seven finals.

Even in a loss, the Pacers sent a message to the rest of the new league. They were going to be a force for years to come. Indiana captured the ABA crown three times in the next four years and reached the Finals again in 1975.

By that time the ABA was dying. Several teams had folded during the league's brief history. Fan support never reached high levels. And the league's games were not on national TV.

Pacers forward George McGinnis, *right*, led the ABA in scoring during the 1974–75 season with an average of 29.8 points per game.

In 1976 the league went out of business. But four successful ABA clubs were asked to join the NBA, including the Pacers, who had won more ABA titles than any other team.

Adjusting to playing in the NBA took time. The Pacers nearly went under before they had the chance. In 1977 the team was on the verge of bankruptcy. Only a TV telethon, hosted by coach and general manager Bobby "Slick" Leonard, raised enough cash to keep the Pacers going. Fans gave what money they could. And many who tuned in bought season tickets. The revenue allowed the team to keep operating.

The Pacers still struggled on the court. Indiana made the playoffs only twice in their first 13 seasons in the new league. It took until the 1993–94 season before the Pacers won an NBA playoff round.

CONTENDERS AGAIN

It wasn't until 1993 and the arrival of coach Larry Brown that Indiana finally found success. The veteran coach helped the Pacers develop a tough, defensive-minded approach.

The Pacers reached the Eastern Conference finals for the first time during the 1993–94 season but lost to the New York Knicks. Indiana was back the next year but could not get past the Orlando Magic.

Brown left after the 1996–97 season, but his winning culture remained. No longer were the Pacers just another struggling NBA team.

NBA legend and Indiana native Larry Bird put together a record of 147–67 in three seasons as the Pacers' head coach in the late 1990s.

The Pacers turned to legendary player Larry Bird to coach the team after Brown's exit. Bird grew up in French Lick, Indiana, about two hours south of Indianapolis. As a player, Bird had led the Boston Celtics to three NBA titles in the 1980s.

Bird brought his winning touch back home with him. The Pacers made it to the Eastern Conference finals in each of his first two seasons. Finally, in 1999–2000, it all came together for Indiana. The team had sharp-shooting guard Reggie Miller knocking down three-pointers. It also featured a rugged defense anchored by forward Dale Davis. The Pacers finally reached the NBA Finals for the first time.

The star-studded Los Angeles Lakers were the last team in Indiana's way. However, massive Lakers center Shaquille O'Neal and superstar guard Kobe Bryant were too much. Los Angeles won the series in six tough games. Miller did his best. He had a chance to tie Game 6 in the final minute, but he missed his attempt at a three-pointer.

It would be as close as Miller and the Pacers would get to their first NBA championship during his Hall of Fame career.

A BLACK EYE FOR THE NBA

Indiana appeared to be a contender going into Miller's final season in 2004–05. The Pacers had won 61 games the season before. Once again they reached the Eastern Conference finals. There they lost to the Detroit Pistons. The games between the Pacers and their archrival Pistons were always physical.

On November 19, 2004, both teams crossed the line. The Pistons were on their way to a 97–82 win at the Palace of

Indiana's Roy Hibbert goes up for a dunk against the Miami Heat during the 2013 Eastern Conference finals.

Auburn Hills in Detroit when things turned ugly. After a fan threw a cup at Indiana star guard Ron Artest, he charged into the stands. A huge brawl broke out between players and fans. The NBA acted swiftly to punish the players involved. The league suspended Artest for the rest of the season. Guard Stephen Jackson and All-Star forward Jermaine O'Neal were also given long suspensions for their roles in the fight.

Promising young guard Tyrese Haliburton came to Indiana as part of a trade with the Sacramento Kings in February 2022.

With Artest out, Indiana lost to Detroit in the second round of the playoffs. Miller headed off into retirement.

MORE CLOSE CALLS

It took the Pacers nearly a decade to return to contention. Indiana made it to the Eastern Conference finals in both the 2012–13 and 2013–14 seasons. The team had versatile forward Paul George. Inside was another stingy defense led by 7-foot-2-inch center Roy Hibbert.

Both times the Miami Heat and superstar LeBron James got in Indiana's way. The underdog Pacers took Miami all the way to Game 7 in 2013. But Miami outscored Indiana 33–16 in the second quarter. The Pacers never recovered. The following year was more of the same. Indiana pushed the defending NBA champion Heat to six games before falling.

Indiana traded George to Oklahoma City in 2017 for guard Victor Oladipo and forward Domantas Sabonis. Oladipo became a star once he arrived in Indiana. With his quick hands, he led the NBA in steals in 2017–18. He made the All-Star team in each of his first two seasons with the Pacers. But Oladipo moved on in 2021 as the team fell out of playoff contention. The Pacers were looking for the next generation of stars to get them back to the top.

Pacers
30

CHAPTER THREE

PRIME PACERS

The Pacers were off to a rough start during their second season in 1968–69. They needed someone to shake things up. Few people around the game loved to do that more than Slick Leonard.

In his 12 seasons coaching the Pacers, Leonard won 529 games. His 387 wins set an ABA record. Star George McGinnis called Leonard a "genius" for the way he could change things on the fly to confuse opposing defenses.

Leonard went on to broadcast games for the Pacers for nearly 30 years. He worked in television first before switching to radio. His signature call was "Boom Baby!" any time Indiana made an important three-pointer.

Leonard's arrival as coach in the late 1960s helped make the Pacers champions. But he walked into a locker room already loaded with talented players. Small forward Roger Brown had

Pacers forward George McGinnis dunks the ball during a game in 1975.

been working at a General Motors plant in Dayton, Ohio, when he tried out for the Pacers. A former high school star in New York City, he made his ABA debut as a 25-year-old in 1967. The smooth shooter went on to average 18.0 points in eight seasons with Indiana. Brown was known as "the Man of 1,000 Moves" for his ability to get to the basket with ease.

While Brown relied on his quickness to make things happen, teammate George McGinnis relied on his strength. "Big George" had little trouble bullying his way to the hoop against weaker opponents. The 6-foot-8-inch, 235-pound McGinnis led the ABA in scoring in 1974–75. He averaged 29.8 points per game while winning the ABA's MVP Award.

Mrs. Slick

The Pacers had a close-knit management team during their first NBA seasons in the late 1970s. While Slick Leonard was the head coach and general manager, his top assistant was his wife, Nancy. It was Nancy Leonard who came up with the idea for the Pacers' 1977 telethon that saved the team from going under.

McGinnis was an Indiana basketball legend even before he suited up for the Pacers. A native of Indianapolis, he was named the state's top high school player as a senior. That season he led his team to a 31–0 record and a state title. He then stayed home for his college career, enrolling at the University of Indiana. At the time, freshmen were ineligible to play college basketball. But McGinnis broke out when he got the chance as a sophomore.

The powerful forward averaged 30 points per game.

Alongside McGinnis inside was center Mel Daniels. Together they formed one of the ABA's best frontcourt tandems. Daniels started playing basketball as a punishment. In high school he skipped gym class for a few weeks. His teacher was also the basketball coach. Daniels was forced to play basketball to make up for his missed classes. Despite never playing before, he quickly became a star.

Bobby "Slick" Leonard spent 50 years with the Pacers as head coach, general manager, and broadcaster.

While McGinnis had no trouble putting up shots, Daniels had no trouble chasing them down. The ABA's all-time leading rebounder led the league three different times.

STELLAR SHOOTERS

The Pacers had trouble winning games during their early years in the NBA. But they had one of the league's best scorers in

Chuck Person was a prolific shooter during his six seasons with the Pacers.

Billy Knight. The guard made the NBA All-Star team during Indiana's first season in the more established league in 1976–77. He averaged 26.6 points a game that year. That total was second in the league behind Hall of Fame guard Pete Maravich of the New Orleans Jazz.

Nobody ever had to tell Chuck Person, also known as "the Rifleman," to shoot the ball. He always thought he was open. Person joined the Pacers in 1986 and quickly made a splash by being named the NBA's Rookie of the Year. The NBA had only put in a three-point line in 1979. Person was one of the first players to take full advantage of it. He never averaged fewer than 17.0 points per game for the Pacers.

REGGIE AND THE DUTCHMAN

After a decade of struggles since joining the NBA, the Pacers' fortunes changed at the 1987 NBA Draft. That day they held the eleventh overall pick. Local fans knew exactly who they wanted. Indiana native Steve Alford had been a star for the Hoosiers of Indiana University. The slick-shooting guard had just won a national championship.

The Pacers instead selected a skinny shooting guard from the University of California, Los Angeles (UCLA) named Reggie Miller. About 5,000 fans showed up at Market Square Arena, the team's home court, to watch the draft. Miller's selection brought a chorus of boos around the building.

It did not take long for Miller to turn the boos into cheers. By his third season, Miller was an All-Star. By the 1993–94 season, Miller was one of the best players in the league. And the Pacers were one of its best teams.

Over the course of his 18 seasons—all of them with the Pacers—Miller became an NBA legend. The skinny 6-foot-7 player's jump shot was tough to block. He would rise high and launch the ball over the outstretched hands of defenders. Miller is considered one of the best pure shooters in basketball history.

During the 1990s, most teams wanted to get the ball inside for easy shots. But Miller had no trouble chucking it from deep. He poured in 2,560 three-pointers during his career, a record at the time of his retirement in 2005.

While Miller was Indiana's "Mr. Outside," Rik Smits was Indiana's "Mr. Inside" from 1988 to 2000. The center grew up in the Netherlands. He didn't start playing basketball until he was 15 years old. His work around the basket earned him the nickname "the Dunking Dutchman." But it was his steady shooting stroke that helped him retire as the second-leading scorer in franchise history behind Miller. Together they helped fuel Indiana's lone NBA Finals appearance in 2000.

Miller and Smits handled most of the scoring for the Pacers in the 1990s. There weren't a lot of shots to go around for the other players. Indiana had gritty role players to fill out the roster. Antonio Davis and Dale Davis were known as "the Davis Brothers." They weren't actually related, but both played with similar determination for rebounding and defense. Point guard

Reggie Miller scored more than 25,000 points in a Pacers uniform. No other Indiana player has more than 13,000.

Forward Antonio Davis was a key bench player for the Pacers in the late 1990s.

Mark Jackson was one of the finest passers of his generation. He led the NBA in assists in 1996–97.

Smits's retirement left the Pacers with a hole in the middle of their roster entering the 2000s. Jermaine O'Neal arrived in a trade with the Portland Trail Blazers to fill it. O'Neal came to the NBA straight from high school but didn't play much in Portland. The Pacers offered him a chance to shine. O'Neal won the NBA's Most Improved Player Award in 2002. He blossomed into one of the league's best power forwards. O'Neal made six straight All-Star teams in the 2000s. He also finished third in the 2004 MVP race. O'Neal lost out only to superstars Kevin Garnett and Tim Duncan.

O'Neal's play made the Pacers contenders in the early 2000s. But he was not alone. Miller was still contributing scoring at the end of his career. And the team had Ron Artest, one of the best defenders in the NBA. The forward, who would later change his name to Metta World Peace, made his only All-Star team during the 2003–04 season. That year his persistent play helped the Pacers put up a 61–21 record.

THE NEW GENERATION

Like O'Neal, Paul George wasn't well known when the Pacers drafted him in 2010. The shooting guard/small forward had played college basketball out of the limelight at Fresno State. George also developed steadily. By 2012–13 he was one of the league's best players. George became popular for his scoring ability and his defense. But he was also tough. George was playing for the US National Team in 2014 when he broke his right leg in an exhibition game. He returned to play at the end of the 2014–15 NBA season.

Forward Paul George made four All-Star teams in seven seasons with the Pacers.

By the following year, George was back in All-Star form. However, his contract was running out at the end of the 2016–17 season. He told the Pacers he wanted to head back to California and sign with the Lakers. Rather than lose him for nothing, Indiana traded him to the Oklahoma City Thunder in the summer of 2017.

The trade that sent George to Oklahoma provided a homecoming to former Indiana University star Victor Oladipo. His return to the Hoosier State gave the Pacers a lightning-quick guard. It also brought a much-needed dose of energy. Oladipo was on the verge of becoming one of the NBA's best young players when a major knee injury in January 2019 sidetracked him. He made it back to the court in 2020, but his days were numbered with the struggling Pacers. Oladipo told the team he planned to become a free agent after the 2020–21 season. The Pacers decided to trade Oladipo to the Houston Rockets in January 2021.

By February 2022, Indiana's roster had turned over completely. The Pacers were rebuilding the roster. They hoped this time the new group could finally bring home an NBA championship.

BROW
35
NETS
35
INDIANA
0

CHAPTER FOUR

PACER PEAKS

Before Reggie Miller and Paul George, there was Roger Brown. The guard didn't start his professional career until he was 25. But Brown played like he was making up for lost time. His greatest performance came during the 1970 ABA Finals.

The Pacers held a 2–1 lead over the Los Angeles Stars entering Game 4. Then Brown took over. He scored 53 points while adding 13 rebounds and six assists in a 142–120 victory. Brown finished the job with 45 points in Game 6. He hit seven three-pointers as Indiana wrapped up the championship.

Sometimes a player like Brown rises to greatness and rescues his team. But often it takes everyone working together to earn a championship. The Pacers were locked in a tough battle with the rival Kentucky Colonels in the 1973 ABA Finals. The Colonels slowed the game down in hopes of flustering the high-flying Pacers. Indiana responded by playing lockdown

Roger Brown, *left*, was a key part of the Pacers' ABA dynasty during the early 1970s.

defense. In the deciding seventh game, Indiana dug in. The Pacers held the Colonels to just 11 points in the third quarter. The 88–81 win gave Indiana its third ABA title in four years.

CAN'T STOP REGGIE

For 18 seasons, Miller burned opponents with his super smooth shooting touch. Often, his shot was at its most dangerous when the team needed it the most. That was the case against the New York Knicks in the 1994 Eastern Conference finals. In Game 5, Miller put on one of the greatest shooting displays in playoff history. His 25 fourth-quarter points rallied the Pacers from 12 points down to win. Miller made all five of his three-point attempts in the quarter.

It would be the first of many thrilling playoff moments for Miller. One year later, Miller famously scored his eight points in 8.9 seconds to lead the Pacers past the Knicks in Game 1 of the 1995 Eastern Conference semifinals. In 1998 the Pacers were locked in a tough series against the two-time defending NBA champion Chicago Bulls. Miller was in a personal scoring battle with Bulls superstar guard Michael Jordan. The Pacers lost the first two games. In Game 3, Miller was playing on an injured ankle. But he still scored 13 of his 28 points in the fourth quarter in a 107–105 Pacers victory. He saved his biggest shot for Game 4. Miller drilled a go-ahead three-pointer with less than one second remaining. The shot held up after Jordan's

Reggie Miller celebrates his last-second basket against the Chicago Bulls in Game 4 of the 1998 Eastern Conference finals.

Pacers guard Jalen Rose, *left*, drives to the basket against the Los Angeles Lakers in Game 5 of the 2000 NBA Finals.

final heave banked off the backboard and spun out of the hoop. Indiana won 96–94.

After years of close losses in the playoffs, Indiana finally reached the NBA Finals in 2000. It was only fitting that the Pacers got there by beating the Knicks. Miller again delivered when it mattered most. In Game 6 of the conference finals, he scored 17 of his 34 points in the fourth quarter. Indiana won 93–80 to clinch the series.

"It's been a long road," guard Jalen Rose said. "We've knocked on the doors a lot of times and now we are in."

The Pacers' run ended there. They lost to the star-studded Los Angeles Lakers in the Finals. Behind Miller and Rose, the Pacers gave the Lakers their best shot. The two guards each averaged at least 23 points in the series, with both playing at least 42 minutes per game. However, Shaquille O'Neal and the Lakers overpowered Indiana. After winning the first two games, Los Angeles went on to claim the series in six.

Fever Pitch

The Pacers received a sister team when the Indiana Fever joined the WNBA in 2000. By 2005 the Fever were playoff regulars. Seven years later they delivered their first league title. Forward Tamika Catchings led the way as Indiana knocked off the Minnesota Lynx 3–1 in the best-of-five championship series. It was the first professional basketball title in Indiana since the Pacers captured their last ABA crown in 1973. It was a crowning moment for Catchings, who also won four Olympic gold medals and a college title in her career.

The Pacers selected sharpshooting guard Chris Duarte, *right*, with the thirteenth pick of the 2021 draft.

GEORGE STEPS UP

Fourteen years later Indiana found itself as an underdog again, this time against the Miami Heat in the 2014 Eastern Conference finals. The Pacers trailed 3–1 heading into Game 5. That's when Paul George took over. George stamped himself as one of the NBA's best young talents with a spectacular performance. He scored 31 of his 37 points in the second half as the Pacers held on for a 93–90 win. The Heat ultimately claimed the series. But George showed Pacers fans he was a worthy heir to Miller as the face of the franchise.

However, George didn't end up following Miller by spending his entire career with the Pacers. After George left the team in 2017, the Pacers looked for new stars. By the end of the 2020–21 season, Indiana was a team in transition. That summer the Pacers drafted sharpshooting guard Chris Duarte from the University of Oregon in the first round.

They added another young player with big potential during the 2021–22 season. Point guard Tyrese Haliburton was the twelfth pick in the 2020 draft by the Sacramento Kings. He joined the Pacers on February 8, 2022, as part of a six-player trade between the two teams. It was one of a handful of moves Indiana made to put a new, young, exciting team on the floor.

To lead the youth movement the Pacers brought back an old coach. Rick Carlisle led Indiana for four seasons in the mid-2000s. In 2003–04 he guided the Pacers to a 61–21 record. With a mixture of new and old faces, the Pacers hoped to write the next chapter in their storied history.

1967

The Indiana Pacers are founded as an original member of the ABA.

1968

Bobby "Slick" Leonard makes his coaching debut for Indiana in a 105–95 loss to the Minnesota Pipers.

1970

The Pacers beat the Los Angeles Stars 111–107 in Game 6 of the 1970 ABA Finals to win the franchise's first championship.

1972

Roger Brown's 32 points help the Pacers edge the New York Nets 108–105 to capture the 1972 ABA Finals in six games.

1973

Playoff MVP George McGinnis pours in 27 points as Indiana tops the Kentucky Colonels 88–81 in Game 7 of the 1973 ABA Finals. It is the franchise's third title in four years.

1976

After the ABA and NBA merge, the Pacers are one of four teams that join the NBA.

1987

The Pacers select shooting guard Reggie Miller out of UCLA with the eleventh overall pick in the NBA Draft.

1993

After four straight seasons of first-round playoff exits, the Pacers hire Larry Brown as head coach.

1994

Behind 31 points from Reggie Miller, Indiana beats the Orlando Magic 99–86 in Game 3 of the first round of the Eastern Conference playoffs, giving the Pacers their first-ever NBA playoff series victory.

1995

Reggie Miller scores eight points in nine seconds against the New York Knicks in Game 1 of the Eastern Conference semifinals. The Pacers eventually defeat New York in seven games before falling to Orlando in the conference finals.

2000

Miller pours in 34 points as the Pacers top the Knicks 93–80 in Game 6 of the Eastern Conference finals. The win clinches Indiana's first-ever appearance in the NBA Finals.

2004

The Pacers finish off their best regular season in franchise history with a 101–96 victory over the Chicago Bulls. Indiana's 61–21 record is the best in the NBA, but the Pacers lose to the Detroit Pistons in six games in the Eastern Conference finals.

2014

Indiana wins its sixth NBA Central Division title by finishing with a 56–26 record. The Pacers fall to Miami in six games in the Eastern Conference finals.

2017

Star forward Paul George tells the team he plans to leave as a free agent. Instead, Indiana trades him to the Oklahoma City Thunder.

2021

Rick Carlisle, who previously coached the team for four seasons from 2003–04 to 2006–07, is rehired before the 2021–22 season.

FACTS

FRANCHISE HISTORY
American Basketball
  Association (1967–76)
National Basketball Association
  (1976–)

ABA CHAMPIONSHIPS
1970, 1972, 1973

KEY PLAYERS
Roger Brown (1967–74, 1975)
Mel Daniels (1968–74)
Dale Davis (1991–2000, 2004)
Paul George (2010–17)
Tyrese Haliburton (2022–)
Freddie Lewis (1967–74,
  1976–77)
George McGinnis (1971–75,
  1980–82)
Reggie Miller (1987–2005)
Jermaine O'Neal (2000–08)
Chuck Person (1986–92)
Rik Smits (1988–2000)

KEY COACHES
Larry Bird (1997–2000)
Larry Brown (1993–97)
Rick Carlisle (2003–07, 2021–)
Bobby "Slick" Leonard
  (1968–80)

HOME ARENAS
Indiana Farmers Coliseum
  (1967–74)
Market Square Arena (1974–99)
Gainbridge Fieldhouse (1999–)
  Formerly known as:
  Conseco Fieldhouse
    (1999–2011)
  Bankers Life Fieldhouse
    (2011–21)

DUNK KINGS

The Pacers have had two players win the Slam Dunk title. Fred Jones won it in 2004, and Glenn Robinson III captured the crown in 2017.

FILLING IT UP

The 1968–69 Pacers averaged 119.6 points per game, a team record that still stands.

IN THE RAFTERS

The Pacers have retired five numbers: No. 30 (George McGinnis), No. 31 (Reggie Miller), No. 34 (Roger Brown), No. 35 (Mel Daniels), and No. 529 (number of coaching wins by Slick Leonard).

ROAD SHOW

Indiana's 152–95 win over the Oklahoma City Thunder on May 1, 2021, was the most lopsided regular-season road victory in NBA history.

THE PACER PANTHER

The Pacers' mascot, a panther nicknamed Boomer, earned a spot in the Mascot Hall of Fame in 2020.

GLOSSARY

assist
A pass that leads directly to a basket.

contention
Among the teams challenging for a championship.

draft
A system that allows teams to acquire new players coming into a league.

foul
Illegal contact with another player during the course of the game.

inbound
To pass the basketball from out of bounds back into play.

playoffs
A set of games played after the regular season that decides which team is the champion.

rebound
To catch the ball after a missed shot.

rookie
A professional athlete in his or her first year of competition.

steal
To take the ball from a player on the other team.

veteran
A player who has played many years.

INFORMATION

BOOKS

Flynn, Brendan. *The NBA Encyclopedia for Kids*. Minneapolis, MN: Abdo Publishing, 2022.

Mahoney, Brian. *GOATs of Basketball*. Minneapolis, MN: Abdo Publishing, 2022.

Ybarra, Andres. *Great Basketball Debate*s. Minneapolis, MN: Abdo Publishing, 2019.

ONLINE RESOURCES

To learn more about the Indiana Pacers, please visit **abdobooklinks.com** or scan this QR code. These links are routinely monitored and updated to provide the most current information available.

INDEX

ABOUT THE AUTHOR

Will Graves has worked for more than two decades as a sports journalist and since 2011 has served as correspondent for The Associated Press in Pittsburgh, Pennsylvania, where he covers the National Hockey League, the National Football League, and Major League Baseball as well as various Olympic sports.